Polish
Proverbs

By
HELEN STANKIEWICZ ZAND

●

1st Printing - 1961
2nd Printing - 1965
3rd Printing - 1970
4th Printing - 1974

●

Published by Polish American Journal
413 Cedar Ave., Scranton, Pennsylvania 18505

───

Printed in U.S.A.

───

Cover Design by Henry Archacki, New York, N.Y.

───

$\mathcal{A}bout$

$\mathcal{T}he$

$\mathcal{A}uthor:$

Photo by Frank Foye from
portrait by Zoltan Heya

HELEN STANKIEWICZ
ZAND was born in Lodz,
Poland, and came to this
country as a child, in 1907,
with her parents. She grew
up in the large Polish community in Buffalo a n d
graduated f r o m Cornell
University, where she was elected to the Phi Beta Kappa and
Phi Kappa Phi societies, and from the University of Buffalo Law
School. A social worker and teacher, she has worked profession-
ally and as a volunteer in Buffalo, Detroit, Rochester, New York
City and Erie.

Since 1947, when she and her family moved to Erie, she has
been a member of the faculty of Gannon College, as lecturer in
Sociology and Polish. She is the translator into English of Stefan
Zeromski's ASHES, published by Alfred A. Knopf in 1928, and
author of numerous articles in the field of Polish folkways which
have appeared in POLISH AMERICAN STUDIES. She has served
as director in many social service and cultural organizations, is a
member and past vice president of the Polish American Historical
Association, and at present a member of the Governor's Com-
mission on Public Library Development in Pennsylvania.

She is the wife of Stephen J. Zand, noted aeronautical en-
gineer and holder of the Presidential Medal of Merit. She has
two children, a son and a daughter, and four grandchildren.

INTRODUCTION

Like all peoples with an agricultural background and a long national tradition, the Poles have a wealth of proverbs dealing with life, fate, the nature of God and man, the elements, the earth - all the philosophical and practical problems of existence. Perhaps Polish proverbs are not so numerous as those of some other nations - the Spaniards or the Portuguese, for example, of whom it has been said that two of them can sit down and talk for hours using only proverbs, or the Germans who have a compilation listing 250,000 proverbs and proverbial expressions. Still, every Pole knows a hundred or two and collectors know many thousands - the celebrated collection of Adalberg contains 40,000. Unlike other nationalities, however, among whom sophistication reduces the use of proverbs, the Poles employ theirs very freely irrespective of class, education, city or country residence, and this is as true now as a hundred years ago - to this day native and foreign saws enliven the speech of all Poles. Moreover, Poles of all classes have a strong tendency to create epigrams, to conclude discussion with a rounded phrase, if not a quoted one then one coined *ad hoc* - doubtless many Polish proverbs arose in this way and more are being added constantly.

The richest source of Polish proverbs is indigenous experience - the countryman's daily struggle with the soil, with weather, with poverty - and the history of the nation which called for patience, faith, endurance. But since up to the middle of the 16th century all writing in Poland was in Latin, and since the classics formed for so long the basis and substance of all education, Greek and Latin sayings entered the language of the upper classes and through them the speech of the people.

Thus all Poles say, *"W zdrowym ciele zdrowy duch,"* "A sound mind in a sound body;" *"Nikt nie jest prorokiem we własnym domu,"* "No one is a prophet in his own house;" *"Głos ludu, głos Boga,"* "The voice of the people is the voice of God;" *"Dojść po nitce do kłębka,"* "Follow the thread to the ball," in reference to the story of Theseus and Ariadne; *"W mętnej wodzie ryby łowić,"* "To fish in troubled waters;" *"drakońskie prawa,"* "Draconian laws." Also, there is a fairly widespread use of proverbs in the original Latin again at all levels - *"Nec Hercules contra plures"* - even Hercules is powerless against superior numbers - is probably known and used by all Poles.

Similarly, since the Poles embraced Christianity in 966, the Scriptures have been part of their life for a thousand years and while, being mainly Catholics, they do not read the Bible as do the Protestants, they know the Holy Writ through their clergy and many scriptural sayings have entered the daily language. Thus we have: *"Niech nie wie lewica, co robi prawica"* - "Let not thy left hand know what thy right hand doeth;" *"Kto mieczem wojuje, ten od miecza ginie"* - "They that take the sword shall perish by the sword;" *"Jak posiejesz, tak zbierzesz"* - "As ye sow, so shall ye reap;" *"Kto wiatr sieje, burzę zbiera"* - "Who sows the wind, reaps the whirlwind." Shorter sayings are even more common: *"Od Annasza do Kaifasza"* - from Annas to Caiphas, referring to the trial of Christ and used in the sense of "from pillar to post," occurs frequently, also *"miska soczewicy"* - a mess of pottage, *"hiobowe wieści"* - Job's news, i.e. news of disaster or misfortune; *"Sodoma i Gomora"* - Sodom and Gomorrha, and many others.

Wars, dynastic changes, migration, military service, enemy occupation, as well as travel, trade and study in foreign countries, have added proverbs of other nations. Thus the Poles share many sayings with the Germans, Russians, Italians, French, English and others. In many cases it is impossible to determine where the saying originated or what nation used it first - like inventions and ideas generally, it is possible that these common sayings arose independently in several places at once, the time and circumstances being ripe for their rise; more probably, their existence in many languages is proof of a common cultural heritage and of age-old and effective contact. Among these universal, or at least pan-European proverbs are *"Pańskie oko konia tuczy"* - "The master's eye fattens the horse;" *"Darowanemu koniowi nie patrz w zęby"* - "Do not look a gift horse in the mouth;" *"Nie wszystko złoto, co się świeci"* - "All that glitters is not gold;" *"Kuj póki żelazo gorące"* - "Strike while the iron is hot;" *"Potrzeba, matka wynalazków"* - "Necessity, the mother of invention;" *"Nowa miotła dobrze zamiata"* - "A new broom sweeps clean;" *"Gość i ryba po trzech dniach cuchnie"* - "Guests and fish stink after three days."

I have included in this collection only those proverbs which, so far as I know, are of purely Polish origin or which constitute an interesting variant of a universal proverb or which, while used also by other nations, are so widely employed in Poland that leaving them out would be felt as a serious omission. My sources are four: my own recollection of the proverbs I heard as a child in the large Polish community in Buffalo in which I grew up; the reading of Polish authors, especially Sienkiewicz; Polish-language textbooks and newspapers and finally friends who, knowing of my interest, sent me their lists of proverbs. Among these I wish to single out for special thanks Mme. Maria Kopera of Cracow, Poland, who sent me a list of over 250 proverbs, a fourth of them dealing with weather and the calendar.

My purpose in compiling this list was not to give an exhaustive treatment of the Polish proverb or even a representative sampling but rather to accomplish three quite different tasks: to indicate, through the modest medium of proverbs, the essential unity of western culture, indeed the universality of all human experience; to furnish an aid to the study of Polish, to new students to some extent but chiefly to those third- or fourth-generation Americans of Polish background who have some knowledge of the Polish language and may find this an easy and pleasant way of strengthening and enlarging it; and finally to provide pleasure to the curious reader who is "involved in mankind" and may find interesting this insight into Polish mentality.

Should any Polish-speaking reader wish to explore the field further, the following two works are available: Jan Stanislaw Bystroń, *Przysłowia Polskie,* (Polish Proverbs), Cracow, 1933, a scholarly but very readable and informative treatise on proverbs generally and on Polish proverbs in particular, tracing their origin and use as a reflection of the culture of the nation; and Julian Krzyżanowski, *Mądrej Głowie Dość Dwie Słowie,* subtitled *Trzy Centurie Przysłów Polskich* (To a Wise Head Two Words Are Sufficient - Three Hundred Polish Proverbs), Warsaw, 1958, a detailed historical analysis of 300 common and less common proverbs, tracing their origin, variants and spread, with an especially valuable review of the work of former collectors beginning with Biernat of Lublin whose work appeared in 1522. Samuel Adalberg, *Księga Przysłów, Przypowieści i Wyrażeń Przysłowiowych Polskich* (Book of Polish Proverbs, Maxims and Proverbial Expressions) published in Warsaw in the years 1888-1894, has been out of print for many years. It is doubtless accessible in the larger libraries in Poland; I do not know of its existence anywhere in the United States.

For the reader interested in proverbs generally, not merely in Polish ones, mention must be made of a library assembled by a Polish collector, Ignacy Bernstein, which may be unique in size and scope: it consists of 4761 volumes, representing all European languages and many Asiatic and African. Among the European are 285 Polish works, 893 German, 566 French, 265 English, 199 Russian, 448 Italian, 193 Spanish, 14 Basque, 10 Gypsy, 5 Albanian, 2 Maltese, 5 Icelandic, 4 Irish. Bequeathed by the collector to the Polish Academy of Sciences (Polska Akademia Nauk) in Cracow, it is accessible to the public ten months of the year. A catalogue of the library, with a foreword in Polish and French and a brief description of each item, was published in Warsaw in 1900 under the title: *Katalog Dzieł Treści Przysłowiowej Składających Bibliotekę Ignacego Bernsteina* (Catalogue of Works Dealing with Proverbs Comprising the Library of Ignacy Bernstein); the Congressional Library and the Library of the University of Illinois both have a copy of it, indexed under: Katalog, Bernstein. I am indebted to the latter for the generous loan of it and to Professor Alexander Turyn of the Classics Department of that university for drawing it to my attention.

In presenting the proverbs, I debated about the arrangement: whether to follow the usual practice and make the list alphabetical according to the key word or words or whether to devise some other way. I felt the work would be more readable if I grouped the proverbs by ideas and general categories rather than individual words. A further argument in favor of this method seemed to me the fact that the metaphor used is seldom a key to what the proverb is about - "As the twig is bent, so grows the tree" is not about twigs or trees but about children.

A note on the translations I offer: since a literal translation often fails to give the humor or special flavor of the expression - indeed may be an actual distortion of it - I have given in most instances, in addition to the translation, an explanatory note or an equivalent proverb in English. Further, in some cases, I have taken the liberty of changing the metaphor or form for the sake of "punch" or rhyme, striving, in all cases, to render the spirit and "feel" of the saying as well as its literal meaning.

A word about the form of Polish proverbs. The majority of them rhyme, sometimes with considerable strain or even complete distortion of a word - native, homespun proverbs especially show no compunction on that score. This results in added humor and pungency but unfortunately, like all play on words, is untranslatable.

In connection with the possible use of this collection as a linguistic aid, I feel I should give a note on the pronunciation of Polish. Despite its forbidding appearance - we must concede that names like Wrzeszcz and Szczebrzeszyn look unpronounceable - Polish is easy to pronounce and to read. It is wholly phonetic, it reads as it's written - "as it stands" the Poles say. There are no silent or slurred letters or syllables, every letter or combination of letters is given its full value in every word. Thus, knowing the Polish alphabet, the sound of certain combinations and the rule about accent, one may read correctly and be understood even without understanding a word of what one is reading. Given a good instructor, this ability may be acquired in a half hour. Lacking an instructor, the following notes may be helpful:

The Polish alphabet has the same letters as the English except that it lacks q, v and x whose sounds are rendered by kł, w and ks respectively. There are additional sounds, however, and these are provided either by certain combinations or by diacritical signs, as noted below.

Vowels: Polish vowels are a, e, i, o, u and y; they are of uniform length and invariable, with sounds as follows:

a as a in father
e as e in bet
i as i in machine; where, however, the i is preceded by a consonant and followed by a vowel, it does not form a separate syllable but serves merely to soften the preceding consonant as in the English words onion, piano.
o as aw in saw
u as oo in poor
y as i in pin

Additional vowels are ó which has the same sound as u above, ą which has the sound of on in song, and ę which has the sound of an in bank.

Consonants: b, f, h, k, l, h, p and t are pronounced exactly as in English.

c = ts except as follows:
        when written ć or when followed by i, it has the sound of the English ch - thus the English words check, cheek, chalk would be written respectively ciek, cik, ciok.
        ch = h

cz = the English ch or tch but somewhat harder and "drier" - produced with clenched teeth, in contrast to ć which is softer, "moister," produced with teeth less tightly closed.

d has the same sound as in English except when followed by a softened z: dź has the sound of dg in ledge; dż and drz have approximately the same sound as dź but harder and "drier" as with ć and cz above. The combination of d and an ordinary z gives the sound of ds or dz in the English words odds, adze, except where it is followed by i - in that case it has the sound of dź above.

g is always hard as in the English words go, get.

j has the sound of the English consonant y as in yet, you.

ł - the so-called crossed l - has the sound of English w.

n has the same sound as in English except when marked with a slanted dash - ń - then it has the sound of the first n in onion.

r is trilled, with the tip of the tongue, as in Scottish speech. r followed by z produces a hard zh as in the French word *gens* with one exception: in the word *marznąć,* to freeze, and its derivatives, the r and z are pronounced separately.

s has the sound of the English s in smooth; when marked with a slanted dash - ś - or followed by an i, it has the sound of s in sugar; when followed by z, the sound is similar to that of ś but, again, "harder and drier," as with ć and cz above.

z has the sound of the English z except when marked with a slanted dash - ź - or followed by an i, marked with a dot or preceded by r, or preceded by c, as indicated above in connection with c, d, and r. Thus ź = z in azure; ż and rz give a sound similar to ź but, again, "harder and drier," more like the French g in *Genevieve, gendarme.*

szcz = the combination shch as in hu*sh*, *ch*ild but, again, "harder and drier" than the English; a softer, more liquid version of the same sound is the combination śé. It may be noted here that the English sounds ch, sh and zh are intermediate in this respect of hardness and softness between the Polish sounds é, ś, ź at the one extreme and cz, sz and rz at the other. The difference is sharply marked in Polish and disregard of it, or inability to articulate it, may lead to humorous confusion, as with *prosię* and *proszę,* the first meaning "little pig," the second "please."

The accent in Polish falls on the penult - the second syllable from the end - except for about a dozen words, mainly of foreign origin, in which it falls on the antepenult. Among these are A-me-ry-ka, A-fry-ka, a-ryt-me-ty-ka, gra-ma-ty-ka, mu-zy-ka. The word *nauka,* science or lesson, permits both accents; when it is used in the sense of science, it is accented on the antepenult: na-u-ka; when it means lesson it may be accented on either the antepenult or the penult but the latter is more common.

H.S.Z.

Gannon College,
Erie, Penna.
Summer 1960.

PROVERBS

Przysłowia są mądrością narodu.
Proverbs are the wisdom of a people.

Na wszystko jest przysłowie.
There is a proverb for everything.

BIRTH

Pod dobrą (złą) gwiazdą się urodził.
He was born under a good (bad) star.
Lucky - unlucky.

★

W czepku się urodził.
He was born in a cap (caul).

The origin of the saying is in the ancient belief that a child coming into the world with a piece of the placenta on his head would be lucky, but the image conveyed by the saying now is a cap. Equivalent to "Born with a silver spoon in his mouth."

CHILDREN

Co rok, to prorok.
Each year a prophet.

Said jocularly of couples who have a child every year. The word *prorok* is used chiefly to rhyme with *rok* but there may be a trace of the belief imputed to Jews that any male child born to a Jewish family may be a prophet or the Messiah.

★

Da Pan Bóg dzieci, da i na dzieci.
God gives children, He will give also for children.

Said in acceptance or resignation by parents when relatives or friends express concern over their growing brood.

Nie daleko pada jabłko od jabłoni.
The apple falls not far from the apple tree.

Much used in Poland though perhaps not of Polish origin since it occurs also in German: *Der Apfel fallt nicht weit vom Stamm.*

★

Jaki ojciec, taki syn.
Like father, like son.

Jaka mać, taka nać.
Like mother, like daughter.

Literally, *nać* means the foliage of vegetables - obviously it is used only to rhyme with *mać* which is an archaic form of *matka*, mother. A closer translation would be "Like root, like plant."

★

Z dobrego gniazda, dobre dzieci.
From a good nest, good children.

★

Czym skorupka za młodu nasiąknie, tym na starość trąci.
What the shell absorbs in youth, of that it will smell in old age.

On the value of good bringing up. "As the twig is bent, so grows the tree."

★

Kto nie słucha ojca, matki, posłucha psiej skóry.
Who does not listen to father, mother, will listen to a dog's hide (i.e. the lash).

★

Jajko mądrzejsze od kury.
The egg is wiser than the hen.

Said ironically of young people who scorn the advice of their elders.

— 11 —

EDUCATION

Czego się Jaś nie nauczył, tego Jan nie będzie wiedział.
What Johnnie has not learned, John will not know.

★

Co bardziej dokuczy, to rychlej nauczy.
What hurts most, teaches soonest.

★

Nieszczęście, przygoda, do rozumu droga.
Ill luck, misadventure, are the way to wisdom.

★

Ciekawość, pierwszy stopień do piekła.
Curiosity, the first step to hell.

An unwise saying, obviously, used to discourage children from asking questions with which parents or teachers can't cope. Equivalent to "Curiosity once killed a cat."

LOVE-COURTSHIP

Niema dalekiej drogi do swej niebogi.
The way is never long to one's beloved.

★

Serce nie sługa.
The heart is not a servant.

Sometimes heard as part of a verse: *Serce nie sługa, nie zna co to pany; nie da przemocą zakuć się w kajdany* - The heart is not a servant, it does not know a master, it will not let itself be chained by force.

★

Krew nie woda.
Blood is not water.

Said in extenuation of heedless falling in love or being carried away by ardor.

★

Kto się lubi, ten się czubi.
Those who like each other, peck at each other.

Lovers will squabble.

— 12 —

Co z oczu, to z serca.
Out of sight, out of heart.

Exact equivalent of "Out of sight, out of mind."

★

Miłość bez pieniędzy, wrota do nędzy.
Love without money, gateway to misery.

★

Każda potwora znajdzie swego amatora.
Every monster will find its admirer.

Said mainly of ill-favored young people who, despite their unattractiveness, find a mate.

MARRIAGE

Jakie wesele, takie życie.
As wedding, so life.

Used as excuse for a lavish wedding, or as a prophecy.

★

Kto się ożeni, ten się odmieni.
Who marries, changes.

Used as encouragement to a girl who hesitates because the suitor has a poor reputation.

WIVES

Dobra żona, mężowa korona.
A good wife is the husband's crown.

Variants are *Oszczędna żona,* a thrifty wife; *Cnotliwa żona,* a virtuous wife.

★

Zła żona, zły sąsiad, diabeł trzeci, jednej matki dzieci.
A bad wife, a bad neighbor, the devil for a third, are all children of one mother.

★

Gdzie ogon rządzi, głowa błądzi.
Where the tail rules, the head blunders.

Biada temu domowi, gdzie krowa dobodzie wołowi.
Woe to the house where the cow butts the ox.

★

Baba z wozu, koniom lżej.
Woman off the wagon lightens the horses' load.

Said when a woman leaves her husband or rejects a suitor.

WOMEN

Gdzie diabeł nie zdoła, babę pośle.
Where the devil can't manage, he'll send a woman.

★

Długo pokuka, kto babę oszuka.
He'll suffer long who a woman did wrong.

RELATIVES

Bliższa koszula ciału niż sukmana.
The shirt is closer to the body than the coat.

A proverb known to many nations in much the same form. The Poles use it most frequently in instances of nepotism - where a relative is favored over a stranger or friend.

★

Na wilka ze szwagrem, na niedźwiedzia z bratem.
Hunt the wolf with a brother-in-law, the bear with a brother.

The bear is considered more dangerous than the wolf, therefore one should hunt him with one's brother whom one can rely on more than a brother-in-law.

★

Ani mi on brat, ani swat.
He's neither brother nor marriage-broker to me.

Neither kith nor kin - said in disclaiming relationship or interest in someone.

— 14 —

MOTHERS

Głos matki, głos Boga.
Mother's voice is God's voice.

★

Droga ta chatka, gdzie mieszka matka.
Dear is the cottage where the mother dwells.

★

Nie ta matka co urodzi, lecz ta co wychowa.
She is not the mother who bears, but the one who rears.

AGE

Nie pamięta wół, jak cielęciem buł.
The ox does not remember when he was a calf.

A very common proverb, used of parents and other oldsters who criticize the young, forgetting how foolish they themselves were when young. An example of distortion for the sake of rhyme - *buł* should be *był*.

★

Stary ale jary.
Old but hale.

Used jocosely, usually of an old man marrying a young woman.

★

W starym piecu diabeł pali.
In an old stove the devil makes the fire.

Said of both men and women who have amorous interests unseemly at their age.

★

Nie pomoże puder, róż, kiedy panna stara już.
Powder and rouge will not help when the maiden is old.

★

Im kot starszy, tym ogon twardszy.
The older the cat, the harder the tail.

— 15 —

LIFE

Jakie życie, taka śmierć.
As life, so death.

Good life, good death; mean life, mean death.

★

Żyć, nie umierać!
Live, not die!

This is the life! This is living! An exclamation of joy.

DEATH

Starość nie radość, śmierć nie wesele.
Old age is not joy, death is not a wedding.

★

Śmierć i żona od Boga przeznaczona.
Death and wife are destined by God.

★

Raz kozie śmierć!
The goat dies but once!

An expression of bravado, or true courage, used in answer to friends who warn one against a dangerous undertaking.

HOME

Wolnoć Tomku w swoim domku.
You're free to do as you please in your own home, Tom.
Szlachcic na zagrodzie równy wojewodzie.
The squire on his close is the equal of the governor.

Both of these proverbs carry the sense of "A man's home is his castle."

★

Chata uboga lecz chędoga.
A cottage poor but clean.

★

Zły to ptak, co własne gniazdo kala.
Evil is the bird that fouls its own nest.

Wszędzie dobrze, lecz najlepiej w domu.
It's fine everywhere, but best at home.

Said usually on returning from a trip or a long visit.

HOSPITALITY

Gość w dom, Bóg w dom.
A guest in the house is God in the house.

★

Czym chata bogata, tym rada.
What the cottage is rich in, that it is happy to share.

Said in a tone of apology for not having more to offer when unexpected guests drop in.

★

Taka droga do Pana Boga jak i do wszystkich świętych.
The way is the same to God as to all the saints.

Said to friends who keep inviting one but do not come themselves. Since visits are valued highly, failure to call is considered an affront and friends are reproached for not calling.

FOOD

Głód najlepszy kucharz.
Hunger is the best cook.

The English version is "Hunger is the best sauce."

★

Gdzie kucharek sześć, tam niema co jeść.
Where there are six cooks, there's nothing to eat.

This is the Polish version of "Too many cooks spoil the broth."

★

Lepiej wydać na piekarza, niż na aptekarza.
Better to spend on the baker than on the druggist.

A reflection of the belief that good and abundant food is the basis of good health.

Tanie mięso psy jedzą.
Cheap meat is eaten by dogs.

Disdain for poor quality, whether in food or in other things.

DRINK

Gdzie się tłucze, leje, tam się dobrze dzieje.
Where things break and spill, there all goes well.

Said to put at ease a guest who breaks a glass or spills wine on a fresh tablecloth but also to express the idea that hospitality, entertaining, are part of the good life.

★

Kto pije, długo żyje.
Who drinks, lives long.

★

Od wódki, rozum krótki.
From drink wits shrink. Literally, "the intelligence is short."

★

Kieliszek wadzi, kieliszek radzi.
The glass antagonizes, the glass advises (i.e. brings discord, but counsel too).

★

Co po trzeźwemu myśli, to po pijanemu powie.
What one thinks when sober, one says when drunk.

In vino veritas! A truth expressed in many tongues.

★

Dobrego karczma nie zepsuje, a złego kościół nie naprawi.
The tavern will not spoil a good man, nor the church mend a bad one.

★

Nie wylewa za kołnierz.
He does not pour it outside his collar.

Used in the sense of "he likes his drink" - usually to correct a statement that someone doesn't drink at all.

FRIENDS

Śród serdecznych przyjaciół psy zająca zjadły.
Amidst cordial friends the dogs ate the hare.

"God protect me from my friends, I can take care of my enemies." The Greeks said, "Be on guard against thy friends."

★

Zjesz beczkę soli, nim poznasz dowoli.
You'll eat a barrel of salt before you know a man thoroughly.

Known to the ancients: Aristotle, Cicero, Plutarch cited it, using various measures: peck, bushel.

COMPANY - TWO OF A KIND.

Z jakim przestajesz, takim się stajesz.
You get to be like your company.

★

Kiedy wejdziesz między wrony, musisz krakać jak i one.
When with crows you go, like them you must caw.

★

Kruk krukowi oka nie wykole.
A raven will not peck out another raven's eye.

This proverb has much the same sense as "Birds of a feather flock together" and "There's honor among thieves."

★

Wart Pac pałaca i pałac Paca.
Potts is worth the palace and the palace Potts.

Pac (pronounced Potts) is a family name; the proverb may have had political connotation at one time but this is now lost - its survival and wide use are doubtless due to its lilting alliteration and rhyme.

Trafiła kosa na kamień.
The scythe hit a stone.

The sense of this proverb is that someone has met his match.

★

Przygania kocioł garnkowi a obydwa smolą.
The pot upbraids the kettle and both smudge.

"The pot calls the kettle black" - universal!

NEIGHBORS

Wiedzą sąsiedzi, jak to siedzi.
Neighbors know how things go (literally, how one sits).

DOING UNTO OTHERS

Nie czyń drugiemu, co tobie nie miło.
Don't do to another what is unpleasant to you.

★

Jaka miarką ty mierzysz, taką ci odmierzą.
What measure you use for others, that they will use for you.

★

Jak Kuba Bogu, tak Bóg Kubie.
As Jacob to God, so God to Jacob.

★

Kto pod kim dołki kopie, sam w nie wpada.
Who digs pits under others falls into them himself.

Based on the Old Testament saying, "Whoso diggeth a pit shall fall therein," Proverbs, xxvi,27.

★

Nie ciesz się, bratku, z cudzego przypadku (upadku).
Do not rejoice, brother, over another's misfortune (fall).

★

Kij ma dwa końce.
A stick has two ends.

Used most commonly as a rejoinder to someone who is threatening one: "You hit me, I'll hit back."

Ręka rękę myje, noga nogę wspiera.
Hand washes hand, leg supports leg.

Usually only the first part of the proverb is used. Equivalent of "Scratch my back and I'll scratch yours."

★

Utopić kogoś w łyżce wody.
To drown someone in a spoonful of water.

The acme of malice and meanness - hating someone so that one would drown him in a spoonful of water.

★

Co było a nie jest, nie pisze się w rejestr.
What was and is not, should not be entered in the register.

Do not hold a man's past against him; let by-gones be by-gones.

SELF-INTEREST

Jeszcze się ten nie urodził, coby wszystkim dogodził.
The man has not yet been born who can please everyone.

★

Kogo nie boli, temu powoli.
If it's not your worry, you don't hurry.

★

Każdy sobie rzepkę skrobie.
Each scrapes his own turnip.

"Every man for himself."

★

Za darmo, boli gardło.
For free, the throat hurts.

No one does anything for nothing - favors must be paid for.

OTHER PEOPLE'S BUSINESS

Nie wtykaj nosa, gdzie nie dałeś grosza.
Don't stick your nose where you've put no penny.

★

Nie kładź palca między drzwi.
Don't put your finger in the door.

CONTENTION - DISSENSION - WAR

Gdzie dwóch się bije, tam trzeci korzysta.
Where two fight, a third profits. "Divide and conquer."

★

Kto nie ma zbroje, niech omija boje.
Who lacks armament should avoid argument.

★

Nie strzelaj prochem kiedy możesz grochem.
Don't shoot with powder when you can shoot with peas.

★

Lepszy żelazny pokój niż złota wojna.
Better an iron peace than a golden war.

★

Rybom woda, ludziom zgoda, bez niej nic.
Water to fish, to men peace - without it, nothing.

ARMY - SOLDIERS

Lepszy żołnierz zbrojny aniżeli strojny.
Better the soldier armed than garbed.

★

Za mundurem panny sznurem.
A uniform on you, the girls will form a queue.

"There's something about a soldier . . ."

OTHER NATIONS

Gdzie kraj to obyczaj.
Other country, other customs.

Used as an expression of tolerance.

Póki świat światem, nie będzie Niemiec Polakowi bratem.
World without end, the German to the Pole will not be
a friend.

★

Zgoda z Niemcami, jak wilkom z barany.
Peace with Germans, as between wolves and sheep.

★

Co Polak to nie Niemiec.
A Pole is not a German.

★

*Węgier, Polak, dwa bratanki: i do korda (szabli) i do
szklanki.*
The Hungarian and the Pole are brothers: with the
sword and with the glass.

★

Szwedy narobiły w Polsce biedy.
Swedes made poverty in Poland.

Folk memory of the Swedish wars against Poland in the
17th century.

★

Gdzie Tatar przejdzie tam trawa nie rośnie.
Where the Tartar passes grass will not grow.

★

Po tatarsku się z kim obejść.
To treat someone in Tartar fashion.

★

Goły jak turecki święty.
Poor as a Turkish saint.

The allusion here is to the poverty of Mohammedan
dervishes. The word *goły* literally means naked or bare.

GOD

Bóg nie rychliwy ale sprawiedliwy.
God is not swift but He is just.

"The mills of the gods grind slowly, but they grind
exceedingly fine."

Pan Bóg cierpliwy ale pamiętliwy.
God is patient but mindful.

★

Strzeżonego Pan Bóg strzeże.
God guards the guarded.

Equivalent to "God helps those who help themselves."

★

Niech Pan Bóg radzi o swojej czeladzi.
Let God look after His servants.

Leave some things to God - don't worry about everything, especially things you can't do anything about or which don't concern you.

★

Chłop strzela lecz Pan Bóg kulę nosi.
Man shoots but God carries the bullet.

Man proposes, God disposes.

FEAR - WORRY

Strach ma wielkie oczy.
Fear has big eyes.

Fear exaggerates danger - things are never so bad as they seem in anticipation.

★

Kto się na gorącym sparzy, na zimne dmucha.
Who is burned on hot, blows on cold.

Once burnt, twice cautious! The proverb exists in various forms in many languages.

★

Z dużej chmury, mały deszcz.
From a big cloud, small rain.

Much ado about nothing - the worry was needless.

★

Koń ma wielki łeb, niech się martwi.
The horse has a large head, let him worry.

Worry is useless.

FATE

Jednemu gody, drugiemu głody.
To one man feast, to another famine.

Not the "feast or famine" in the sense of the English proverb but rather that fate provides joy for one, sorrow for another.

★

Kto bywa na wozie, bywa i pod wozem.
Who is on the wagon will at times be under the wagon too.

The proverbial "ups and downs" which all must be prepared to take.

★

Co ma wisieć, nie utonie.
What is to hang will not drown.

Common to most European languages in the form "He that is to hang will not drown." In Polish the application is not only to persons but to things, in the sense that sooner or later things are righted or that nothing is lost by waiting.

★

Co ma być, będzie.
What is to be will be.

★

Gdyby człowiek wiedział, że się przewróci, to by się położył.
If one knew that he would fall, he would lie down.

Can't go against one's fate; also Hindsight is better than foresight."

EXTREMITY

Tonący brzytwy się chwyta.
The drowning man catches at a razor.

The Italians say the same thing. The English form is "The drowning man catches at straws."

DEVIL

Nie taki diabeł straszny jak go malują.
The devil is not so frightful as he is painted.

The English and German proverbs say "not so black" -
the Italian "not so ugly." The French say "Don't make
the devil blacker than he is."

★

Masz, diable, kaftan.
Here, Satan, is a jacket for you.

Here is a pretty kettle of fish - said in perplexity at an
unexpected and unpleasant turn of events.

LUCK - GOOD AND BAD

Lepszy łut szczęścia niż funt złota.
Better an ounce of luck than a pound of gold.

★

Lepszy łut szczęścia niż cetnar rozumu.
Better an ounce of luck than a hundredweight of wisdom.

★

Jednemu szydła golą, drugiemu i brzytwy nie chcą.
For one awls shave, for another razors won't.

★

Jak szczęście dogrzeje, i kapłon zapieje.
If luck casts a glow, a capon will crow.

★

Jednemu byk się ocieli, a drugiemu krowa nie chce.
For one a bull will calve, for another a cow won't.

★

Nie każdemu skrzypce grają.
The violin does not play for everyone.

★

Jak Pan Bóg dopuści, to i z kija wypuści.
If God permits, a stick will bud.

★

Przybądź szczęście, rozum będzie.
Come luck and wisdom will follow.

I mądry głupi gdy po nędza złupi.
Even the wise man is foolish when misfortune strips him.

★

Więcej szczęścia niz rozumu.
More luck than brains.

The thought that luck is an essential ingredient of success is expressed in many proverbs in many languages. The most common English one is perhaps "Give a man luck and cast him in the sea."

FORTUNE-TELLING - DREAMS

Różnie babka wróżyła.
Variously the old woman foretold.

★

Sen mara, Bóg wiara.
Dream is delusion, God is faith.

Both of the above proverbs express the thought that fortune tellers and dream books should not be relied on.

WEALTH

Pieniądz dobry sługa lecz zły przewodnik.
Money is a good servant but a poor guide.

★

Jak się zwał, tak się zwał, aby się dobrze miał.
No matter what his name, provided he's well off.

★

Zanim tłusty schudnie to chudy umrze.
Before the fat man grows thin, the thin man will die.

POVERTY

Kto ma księdza w rodzie, tego bieda nie ubodzie.
He who has a priest in the family will not be butted by poverty.

★

Biednemu wiatr w oczy wieje.
The wind blows in a poor man's eyes.

Na złamane drzewo wszystkie kozy lezą.
All the goats crawl on a broken tree.

★

Na pochyłe drzewo kozy skaczą,
Goats jump on the bent tree.

★

Gdzie cienko, tam sie rwie.
Where it's thin, there it breaks.

Much the same sense as the three proverbs just above.

★

Kto boso chodzi, nikomu nie szkodzi.
Who walks barefoot hurts no one.

★

Jednym koniem się nie dorobi.
You can't make a fortune with one horse.

CLASS

Kiedyś grzyb, to leź w kosz.
If you are a mushroom, go into the basket.

★

Kiedyś kozieł, idź do chlewu.
If you're a goat, go into the pen.

★

Za wysokie progi na moje nogi.
The threshold's too high for my feet.

★

Nie dla psa kiełbasa.
The sausage is not for the dog.

Heard also as part of a verse:
Nie dla psa kiełbasa, nie dla kota szperka -
Nie dla ciebie, chamie, sołtysowa córka.
The sausage is not for the dog, not for the cat the fat,
Nor for you, churl, the bailiff's daughter.

★

Co mi po tytule, gdy pustki w szkatule.
What good is a title to me when the coffer's empty.

INFLUENCE - LACK OF IT

Wolno psu na Pana Boga szczekać, nie wolno mu Go ugryźć.
A dog may bark at God but may not bite Him.

★

Psie głosy nie idą w niebiosy.
Dogs' cries do not reach the skies.

★

Pies szczeka, wiatr niesie.
Dog barks, wind carries.

★

Pies szczeka, kareta jedzie.
Dog barks, carriage rides on.

All these proverbs convey the sense that you have to be "somebody" to be heard.

DRESS - APPEARANCES

Zastaw się, a postaw się.
Go into debt but make a good showing.

★

Jak cię widzą, tak cię piszą.
As they see you so they describe you.

★

Nie suknia zdobi człowieka ale człowiek suknię.
'Tis not the gown adorns the man but man the gown.

★

Ni aksamit ni atłasy nie dodaczą ci okrasy.
Neither velvet nor satin will add luster to you.

★

Choć suknia szara, byle cnota cała.
Let the gown be gray, so long as virtue's whole.

★

Choć bez kontusza, ale dobra dusza.
Without a *kontusz*, but a good soul.

Poor but honest. The *kontusz* was a type of coat worn by the gentry from the 16th to the 18th century.

SELF-ESTEEM - MODESTY

Siedź w kącie, znajdą cię.
Sit in a corner, they'll find you.

True worth will be recognized.

★

Nie święci garnki lepią.
'Tis not the saints who make pots.

Said in encouragement to persons who lack confidence
in themselves, who are afraid to undertake something
new - the sense of the proverb is that the work of the
world is done by ordinary people like ourselves.

★

Każda liszka swój ogon chwali.
Every vixon praises her own tail.

★

Każdy dudek ma swój czubek.
Every hoopoe has his crest.

The word *dudek* also means fool - in fact this is the usual
connotation of it, as in the saying *Wystrychnąć kogoś na
dudka* - to make a fool of somebody. Both of the above
proverbs are used to express the belief that everyone,
even the humblest, has something to be proud of and
that it is only natural and proper for him to have a
sense of his own worth.

WORK - AMBITION - WILL

Bez pracy niema kołaczy.
Without work there is no bread.

★

Pieczone gołąbki nie lecą same do gąbki.
Roast pigeons do not fall into the mouth by themselves.

★

Módl się i pracuj a będziesz zbawiony.
Pray and work and you shall be saved.

The Latin *"Ora et labora."*

Jaka praca, taka płaca.
As the work is, so the pay.
★
Koniec wieńczy dzieło.
The end crowns the deed.
★
Koniec dzieło chwali.
The end praises the deed.

The completion of a task deserves praise, not the beginning.
★
Nie ten majster kto zaczął ale ten kto skończył.
He is not the master who started but he who finished.

PRESUMPTION

Daj kurze grzędę a ona ci powie, jeszcze wyżej będę.
Give the hen a roost and she'll say "I'll be higher yet."
★
Głaszcz ty kotowi skórę, a on ogon w górę.
Stroke the cat's hide and his tail goes up.
★
Puść świnię w grzędy, a ona się pcha wszędy.
Let the pig into the garden and she'll push herself everywhere.

All of these proverbs express the idea of "Give him an inch and he'll take an ell." The proverb occurs in many languages with varying metaphors.

WILL - WAY

Dla chcącego, nic trudnego.
To the willing one, nothing is difficult.
★
Złej tanecznicy fartuszek zawadza.
A poor dancer will call her apron a hindrance.

Kto chce psa uderzyć, kija znajdzie.
Who wants to hit a dog will find a stick.

Like the preceding one, this proverb is sometimes used in the sense of "Where there's a will, there's a way" but more often to express the idea that if someone wants to find fault with somebody he'll find a pretext.

MASTERS - RULERS

Jaki pan, taki kram.
As master, so shop.

★

Kazał pan, zrobił sam.
The master ordered, did it himself.

Kazał pan, musiał sam.
The master ordered, had to (do it) himself.

The meaning of the above proverbs - heard in both forms - is that overbearing people are sometimes humbled, also that, under the press of necessity, people will do their own work.

★

Pańskie oko konia tuczy.
The master's eye fattens the horse.

An ancient proverb known to many nations.

★

Kto źle rozkazuje, nie długo panuje.
Who commands poorly rules not long.

★

Niema większego tyrana jak z chłopa pana.
There is no greater tyrant than a churl turned earl.
(lit. than a peasant turned master.)

★

Łaska pańska na pstrym koniu jeździ.
A master's favor rides on a piebald horse.

Is spotty, cannot be relied on.

Czego panowie nawarzą, tym się poddani poparzą.
What the lords brew, their subjects will rue (lit. get burned on).

★

Poznać pana po cholewach.
You can tell a gentleman by his boot-tops.

While boot-tops are specified, the proverb is used to express the idea that you can always tell a gentleman.

THRIFT

Ziarnko do ziarnka, a będzie \ (zbierze się) miarka.
Speck to speck and there'll be a peck.

Literally "Grain to grain and there'll be a measure."

★

Grosz do grosza, kupi się kokosza.
Penny to penny and you'll buy a henny.

★

Oszczędnością i pracą ludzie się bogacą.
With thrift and work people grow rich.

A modern, cynical version of this is *Szachrajstwem, nie pracą, ludzie się bogacą* - "By crookedness, not work, people grow rich."

★

Skąpy dwa razy traci.
The miser loses twice.

This does not seem to hold any deep philosophical thought such as is expressed in "It is more blessed to give than to receive" but rather the more mundane idea that the unduly cautious, calculating person is likely to overdo and so lose.

TIME

Czas to pieniądz.
Time is money.

★

Czas płaci, czas traci.
Time pays, time loses.

★

Czas nie zwleka, czas ucieka, nie wiadomo co nas czeka.
Time flies, tarries not, what awaits us we know not.

★

Czas ucieka, wieczność czeka.
Time flies, eternity waits.

★

Kto rano wstaje, temu Pan Bóg daje.
Who rises early, to him God gives.

"Early to bed and early to rise, makes a man healthy, wealthy and wise."

★

Nim słońce wzejdzie, rosa oczy wyje.
Before the sun rises, the dew will eat out your eyes.

Even sunrise is late - the truly industrious person must get up before dawn.

★

Kto pierwszy, ten lepszy.
The first, the better.

First come, first served!

★

Kto późno przychodzi, sam sobie szkodzi.
Who comes late, harms himself.

★

Lepiej późno niż nigdy.
Better late than never.

A very ancient proverb, known to all nations.

★

Co się odwlecze, to nie uciecze.
What is put off will not make off.

Nie od razu Kraków zbudowano.
Krakow was not built all at once.

★

Powoli, a dowoli.
Slowly but sufficiently. Slow but sure.

★

Co nagle, to po diable.
What is done suddenly is worth the devil. Haste makes waste.

★

Nie zawsze Świętego Jana, jest też Szczepana.
It's not always St. John's, there's also St. Stephen's.

It's not always holiday - one can't play all the time - there is a proper time for everything.

★

Komu w drogę, temu czas.
For him who must journey, 'tis time to start.

Said by a departing guest who is reluctant to leave or by a parent or relative who must urge the voyager on but grieves to see him go.

WASTE OF TIME - INEFFECTUAL GESTURES - FUTILITY

Przelewać z pustego w próżne.
To pour from empty to void (i.e. from one empty vessel into another).

To talk without point or purpose, endlessly.

★

Strzelać bez prochu.
To shoot without powder.

Said of assertions without foundation.

★

Kiwać palcem w bucie.
Twiddle toe in boot.

Said especially of empty threats.

— 35 —

Wymierzać się motyką na słońce.
Shake a hoe at the sun.

★

Gniewa się baba na targ, a targ o tym nie wie.
The woman is angry with the market, the market knows nothing about it.

★

Rzucać grochem o ścianę.
Throw peas against the wall.

Wasted effort - the peas will bounce back. Talk falling on deaf ears.

★

Mów wilkowi pacierz, a on woli kozią macierz.
Say prayers to the wolf, he'll still prefer the goat's dam.

★

Budować zamki na lodzie.
Build castles on ice.

★

Myśleć o niebieskich migdałach.
To think of heavenly (blue) almonds.

To day-dream.

★

Szukać wiatru w polu.
To seek the wind in the field.

★

Nie pchaj rzeki, sama płynie.
Don't push a river, it flows by itself.

The sense is that of "easy does it" - patience, moderation.

★

Potrzebny jak piąte koło u wozu.
As necessary as a fifth wheel on the wagon.

In our motor age, this proverb may lend itself to the opposite interpretation: one young acquaintance of the writer took it to mean "As necessary as a spare wheel on a car," i.e. essential, or at least highly desirable.

Potrzebny jak dziura w moście.
As necessary as a hole in the bridge.

Completely useless. New Yorkers say "You need it like a hole in the head."

★

Z pustego nie naleje.
One can't pour from an empty vessel.

Much the same meaning as "You can't get blood out of a stone" (or a turnip) except that it doesn't carry the connotation of hard-heartedness or miserliness but rather mere impossibility.

BUSINESS DEALINGS - ACCOUNTING

Powiedziały jaskółki, że nie dobre są spółki.
The swallows said that partnerships are bad.

★

Dobre rachunki robią dobre stosunki.
Good accounts make good relations.

★

Kochajmy się jak bracia, liczmy się jak Żydzi.
Let us love one another like brothers but make accounts like Jews.

★

Od gęsi owsa się nie kupuje.
One doesn't buy oats from geese.

One doesn't deal with persons who have a conflict of interest or who don't want to sell.

★

Robić rachunki bez gospodarza.
To make accounts without the host.

To plan without the person most concerned. A widely-used proverb; the English, French and Italians say, "He who reckons without the host must reckon twice."

— 37 —

BORROWING - LENDING

Nie pożyczaj, dobry zwyczaj.
Neither borrow nor lend, a custom to commend.

★

Choć pożyczysz choćby złoty, będziesz miał kłopoty.
Though you borrow but a zloty, you'll have trouble.

Don't borrow, don't sorrow!

GIVING

Kto daje i odbiera, ten się w piekle poniewiera.
Who gives and takes back, leads a wretched existence in hell.

Indian giver!

★

Prędka odmowa, datku połowa.
A quick refusal is half a gift.

PROFLIGACY - GAMBLING

Kto rad gra w karty, miewa łeb obdarty.
Who likes to play cards has a ragged head (i.e. goes in rags).

★

Nie graj, Wojtek, nie przegrasz portek.
Don't gamble, Voyteck, and you won't lose your pants.

★

Usiadłeś do wista, gotuj złotych trzysta.
You sat down to play, have money on the way!

Literally, you sat down to whist, prepare three hundred zlotys.

★

Kto na loterii wygra, ten się z diabłem podzieli.
Who wins at lottery, will share with the devil.

— 38 —

FOLLY - FOOLS

Głupich nie sieją, sami się rodzą.
Fools are not sown, they spring up by themselves.

★

Za jednego kpa, będzie innych dwa.
For every fool there will be two more.

★

Głupi i w aptece rozumu nie kupi.
The fool can't buy wisdom even in a drugstore.

★

Co głupiemu po rozumie?
What use is wisdom to a fool?

There is no cure for a fool - he wouldn't know what to do with wisdom.

★

Każdy głupi ma swój rozum.
Every fool has his wisdom.

★

Każda sowa głupia w dzień.
Every owl is stupid in the daytime.

★

Uczył Marcin Marcina, a sam głupi jak świnia.
Martin taught Martin though he's stupid as a pig himself.

Used in contempt of a person who presumes to give advice but is a fool himself.

★

Nadzieja, matka głupich.
Hope, the mother of fools.

★

Obiecanka, cacanka, a głupiemu radość.
A promise is a pretty thing, makes the fool rejoice.

★

I głupi się przydadzą, byle poczciwi i pod mądrych władzą.
There's use for fools, provided they're virtuous and under wise men's rules.

Poznać głupiego po śmiechu jego.
You can tell the fool by his laugh.

Ecclesiastes spoke of the laughter of the fool (vii,6);
proverbs much like the Polish exist in Latin, Italian,
French and English.

FALLIBILITY

Koń ma cztery nogi a potknie się.
A horse has four legs yet will stumble.

Why blame a man for stumbling when he has only two?
Said in excuse of small mistakes.

★

Kto nie ma w głowie, ten musi mieć w nogach.
Who hasn't it in the head, must have it in the feet.

Said in connection with failure of memory rather than
stupidity.

WISDOM

Szkoda, przygoda, do mądrości droga.
Loss, misadventure, are the way to wisdom.

Another form of this is *Nieszczęście, przygoda, do rozumu droga,* listed under EDUCATION.

★

Mądry Polak po szkodzie.
Wise is the Pole when the damage is done.

Another form of this is *Mądry chłop po szkodzie* - Wise
is the peasant after the damage is done. A very ancient
reflection, expressed in many ways.

★

Bywał Janek u dworu, wie jak w piecu palą.
Johnnie has been at court, he knows how stoves are fired.

— 40 —

Mądrej głowie dość dwie słowie.
To a wise head two words are sufficient.

This form of the proverb involves a distortion to effect a rhyme with *głowie*; the correct form would be *dwa słowa*. One also hears *po słowie* (after one word) which is correct grammatically.

★

Mądry głupiemu ustępuje, a głupi się z tego raduje.
The wise man yields to the fool and the fool rejoices over it.

★

Lepiej z mądrym przegrać, niż z głupim wygrać.
Better to lose with a wise man than to win with a fool.

Heard also in the form . . . *zgubić* . . . *znaleźć* - Better to lose with a wise man than to find with a fool.

PATIENCE

Ile kto ma cierpliwości, tyle ma mądrości.
So much as one has of patience, so much has he of wisdom.

★

Lepiej dzwigać niż ścigać.
Better bear (a burden) than pursue.

Used also in the sense "Better dress too warm than not warm enough."

SUFFERING

Nikt nie wie co kogo boli.
No one knows what hurts another.

MODERATION - LACK OF IT

Ostrożnie i wedle miary szafuj słowa i talary.
Carefully and with measure deal out words and treasure.

★

Zbytek kazi pożytek.
Excess fouls use.

★

Za dużo dwa grzyby w barszcz.
Two mushrooms in the soup are too much. "Enough is enough."

★

Nie przebieraj miarki.
Don't overfill the measure. Don't overdo.

★

Robić z igły widły.
To make a pitchfork out of a needle.

Equivalent to "making a mountain out of a molehill."

★

Z żartem jak ze solą, nie przesadź bo bolą.
With jest as with salt: don't overdo for they hurt.

★

Od przybytku głowa nie boli.
The head does not ache from increase (plenty).

★

Lepiej dmuchać niż chuchać.
Better blow on hot than breathe on cold.

The Polish words *dmuchać* and *chuchać* have no exact equivalents in English - *dmuchać* means to blow as on hot food, *chuchać* to breathe warm air as into cold hands. The sense of this proverb and of the one above is "better too much than too little."

GARRULITY - GOSSIP - SILENCE

Jest to cnota nad cnotami, trzymać język za zębami.
It's a virtue above all virtues, to keep one's tongue behind one's teeth.

Słowo wylata wróblem, a powraca wołem.
The word flies out a sparrow, but comes back an ox.

★

Cicho, jak makiem zasiał.
Still, as though sown with poppy seed.

The origin of the proverb may be in the somniferous quality of opium but the sense now is merely that of quiet, silence.

★

Ugryźć się w język.
To bite one's tongue.

Stop talking before one says something one might regret.

★

Gadu, gadu, a chłop śliwki rwie.
Talk, talk, while the man picks the plums.

Said in regret when a person realizes that it's time to end a pleasant chat - "Time's awasting, back to work!"

TRUTH

Prawda w oczy kole.
Truth pricks the eyes.

★

Kto o prawdzie dzwoni, ten o guza goni.
Who proclaims the truth, asks for a bump on the head.

★

Uderz w stół, nożyce się odezwą.
Strike the table, the scissors will speak out.

Truth will out - a guilty person will give himself away.

★

Na złodzieju czapka gore.
The thief's cap is ablaze.

The guilty person cannot hide his guilt - some telltale action will give him away.

Głodnemu chleb na myśli.
The hungry man thinks of bread.

Used when someone makes a Freudian slip or keeps returning to a subject thus revealing what is on his mind.

★

Wyszło szydło z worka.
The awl came out of the bag.

Truth did out.

UNTRUTH - FALSE IMPRESSIONS

Cicha woda brzegi rwie.
Still water tears its banks.

Used in a more derogatory sense than "Still water runs deep."

★

Krowa co dużo ryczy mało mleka daje.
A cow that moos much gives little milk.

★

Wiatrem podszyty.
Lined with wind.

A wind-bag, braggart, liar, unrealiable person.

FANTASY - TALL TALES

Bajka o żelaznym wilku.
A fairy story about an iron wolf.

★

Pleść koszałki, opałki.
To talk nonsense, to lie.

★

Pleść jak najęty.
To talk as though one were hired to do it.

— 44 —

CONDUCT OF LIFE - CONSEQUENCES

Gdyby kózka nie skakała, toby nóżki nie złamała.
If the little goat did not jump, she would not break her leg.

Often used of girls who "get in trouble."

★

Kto w ul dmuchnie, temu pysk spuchnie.
He who blows into a hive will have a swollen face.

Literally *pysk* means muzzle or snout; when used in reference to a person, it is offensive or vulgar, or, as here, humorous.

★

Miłe złego początki lecz koniec żałosny.
Pleasant are the beginnings of evil but the end is sad.

★

Jak sobie pościelesz, tak się wyśpisz.
As you make your bed, so you will sleep.

★

Jakiegoś piwka nawarzył, takie wypij.
Such beer you brewed, such you must drink.

★

Łapał wilk owce, złapano i wilka.
The wolf caught sheep, the wolf was caught too.

★

Nosił wilk, ponieśli i wilka.
The wolf carried away, they carried the wolf away.

★

Przyszła kryska na Matyska.
Came Matysek's turn.

Kryska is a distortion of *kreska*, meaning line or dash. The sense of the proverb is that sooner or later a man's misdeeds catch up with him.

★

Im dalej w las, tem gęściej drzew.
The farther into the woods, the thicker the trees.

Involvement deepens as we proceed.

Tak długo dzban wodę nosi, dopóki się ucho nie urwie.
The pitcher carries water until the ear breaks off.

A proverb known to many nations in much the same
form.

★

Gdzie drwa rąbią, tam drzazgi lecą.
Where they chop wood, chips fly.

★

Niema dymu bez ognia.
There is no smoke without fire.

An ancient observation, expressed in many tongues.

BETTER WITH WORSE - "ILL WIND"

Niema złego bez dobrego.
There is no evil without good.

★

Niema takiego złego coby na dobre nie wyszło.
There is no evil that does not bring good.

"It's an ill wind that blows nobody good."

★

Niema róży bez kolców.
There is no rose without thorns.

CONTENTMENT - ACCEPTANCE

Lepszy rydz niż nic.
Better a mushroom than nothing.

★

Na bezrybiu i rak ryba.
When fish are few, a crab will do.

★

Dobra i mucha, gdy wpadnie do brzucha.
Even a fly is good if it falls into the stomach.

Mouse, louse, half a loaf, have been used at various
times in various climes to express the thought that
something is better than nothing.

— 46 —

Lepszy wróbel w garści, niż gołąb na dachu.
Better a sparrow in the fist than a pigeon on the roof.

Lepszy wróbel w ręku, niż cietrzew na sęku.
Better a sparrow in the hand than a heath-hen on a knot.

Lepszy wróbel w ręku, niż kanarek na dachu.
Better a sparrow in the hand than a canary on the roof.

Three Polish variants of the "bird in the hand" known at least since Aesop.

LEAVING WELL-ENOUGH ALONE

Nie budź licha kiedy śpi.
Don't rouse evil (the devil) when it is sleeping.

★

Nie miała baba kłopotu, kupiła sobie prosię.
The old woman had no trouble so she bought herself a young pig.

★

Czego oczy nie widzą, sercu nie żal.
What the eyes see not, the heart craves not.

★

Skoczyć z deszczu pod rynnę.
To jump out of the rain under the rain-spout.

Equivalent to "out of the frying-pan into the fire." The thought has been expressed through many different images by various peoples.

VARIOUS COMPARISONS - PROVERBIAL EXPRESSIONS

Taki z niego będzie ksiądz, jak z diabła kościelny.
He's as fit to be a priest as the devil is to be a sexton.

Said when an obviously unfit youth aspires to the priesthood or is being pushed into it by his family.

Chłop jak dąb.
A man like an oak.

★

Chłopak jak świeca.
A youth like a candle (tall, straight, clean, bright).

★

Dziewczyna jak łania.
A girl like a doe (beautiful, graceful, gentle).

★

Koniec z końcem wiązać.
To tie end with end.

To make ends meet.

★

Jeść aż się uszy trzęsą.
To eat so that one's ears shake.

To eat greedily or with relish; said kindly, most often of children.

★

To nie chodzi pieszo.
This doesn't go on foot.

Used in the sense "not be sneezed at" - small sums of money, opportunities, etc.

★

Ni pies ni wydra, coś w formie świdra.
Neither dog nor otter, something in the shape of a drill.

Equivalent to "Neither fish nor fowl nor good red herring." Usually only the first part of the saying is used.

★

Groch z kapustą.
Peas with cabbage.

A traditional Christmas eve dish but when the phrase is used as a saying it means the height of disorder, confusion, things mixed as are the peas and cabbage in the dish.

— 48 —

Cienko śpiewać.
To sing thinly.

Said of a person who once "talked big" and is now talking small, "eating humble pie."

★

Oczy mydlić komuś.
To soap someone's eyes.

To try to deceive, to "pull wool over someone's eyes."

★

Obwijać w bawełnę.
To wrap in cotton.
To speak euphemistically, to mince matters.

DAYS - WEATHER - CALENDAR

Jaki piątek, taki świątek.
As Friday, so Sunday.

The word *świątek* does not exist in the language except in its plural form in the expression *Zielone Świątki* (literally "the green holidays") - Whitsuntide. The singular form is used here for the sake of rhyme with *piątek* and the sense is that of "Sunday." The reference is to weather rather than to conduct or events.

★

Kto się w piątek śmieje, a w sobotę śpiewa, ten niech się w niedzielę zmartwienia spodziewa.
Who laughs on Friday and sings on Saturday may expect grief on Sunday.

The Poles have a strong feeling about the unseemliness of gayety on Friday.

★

Deszcz ranny, płacz panny, nie długo trwają.
Morning rain, maiden's tears, last not long.

★

Nowy Rok jaki, cały rok taki.
As the New Year, so the whole year.

— 49 —

Na Nowy Rok przybywa dnia na zajęczy skok.
On New Year's the day grows longer by a hare's leap.

★

Bój się w styczniu wiosny, bo marzec zazdrosny.
Beware of spring in January, for March is jealous.

★

Kiedy luty, sporządź buty, bo wnet przyjdą deszcze, pluty.
When it's February, mend your boots, for soon will come rains and floods.

★

Gdy na Gromniczną mróz, szykuj chłopie wóz, a jak lanie to sanie.
If there's frost on Candlemas, prepare the wagon, man; if rain, the sleigh.

This contradicts the almost universal belief, held also in Poland, that a sunny Candlemas forecasts more winter:

Gdy słońce świeci jasno na Gromnicę, to przyjdą większe mrozy, śnieżyce.
If sun shines bright on Candlemas, more frost and snow will this way pass.

The role of the ground hog in connection with Candlemas Day is unknown in Poland. In its place, as in France and Germany, is the bear:

Na Gromnicę niedźwiedź budę swoją poprawia albo też rozrzuca.
On Candlemas the bear either mends his lair or knocks it down.

★

Gdy mróz w lutym ostro trzyma, będzie bardzo krótka zima.
If frost holds fast in February, the winter will not tarry.

Literally, 'will be very short."

Od Świętej Agaty, będą wylatywać muchy za łaty.
From St. Agatha's on, the flies will be flying out through the battens.

St. Agatha's falls on February 5th.

★

Świętej Dorocie uschnie koszula na płocie.
St. Dorothy's shirt will dry on the fence.

St. Dorothy's falls on February 6th. Days are windy, warmer, sunnier.

★

Święty Maciej zimę traci, albo ją bogaci.
St. Matthew either loses the winter or enriches it.

St. Matthew's is February 24th - a crucial day, apparently, as the next proverb also says:

Gdy Święty Maciej lodu nie stopi, długo będą chuchali w zimne ręce chłopi.
If St. Matthew does not melt the ice, peasants will be warming their hands with their breath for a long time.

★

W marcu jak w garncu.
In March as in a kettle.

A little of everything - churning and turning.

★

Marzec to figlarzec.
March is a trickster.

★

Marzec zielony, niedobre plony.
Green March, poor harvest.

★

Jeśli starzec przeżył marzec, będzie zdrów; jeśli baba w maju słaba, pacierz zmów.
If the old man has lived through March, he'll be well; if the old woman is feeble in May, your prayers say.

Na Świętego Grzegorza, idzie zima do morza.
On St. Gregory, the winter goes down to the sea.

St. Gregory's falls on March 12th.

★

Święty Józef kiwnie brodą, idzie zima nadół z wodą.
St. Joseph shakes his beard, see, the winter's disappeared.

Literally, "goes down with the water." St. Joseph's Day
is March 19th.

★

Prima Aprilis, nie patrz bo się omylisz.
April first, do not look for you'll be fooled.

★

*Kwiecień, plecień, wciąż przeplata, trochę zimny, trochę
lata.*
April weaves a dappled pleat, a little cold, a little heat.

★

Deszcz w Wielki Piątek, zapełnia każdy kątek.
Rain on Good Friday, brings a good harvest.

Literally, "fills every corner."

★

Pogody kwietniowe, słoty majowe.
Fair April, wet May.

★

*Jeżeli w kwietniu pszczoły nie latają, to długie chłody
się zapowiadają.*
If in April bees don't fly, lingering cold they prophesy.

★

*Ile razy przed Wojciechem zagrzmi na pola, tyle razy
po Wojciechu zabieli się rola.*
As many times as it thunders o'er the fields before St.
Adalbert, so many times will the soil be white after.

St. Adalbert's Day falls on April 23rd.

★

*Kiedy z Janem przyjdą deszcze, to sześć niedziel kropi
jeszcze.*
If rains come with St. John, six more weeks 'twill rain on.

June 24th is St. John's Day.

Jeśli na Marka żaba się odzywa, to ciepła wiosna rychło przybywa.
If frogs are heard on St. Mark's Day, a warm spring is soon on the way.

St. Mark's falls on April 25th.

★

Deszcz w Święty Marek, ziemia jak skwarek.
Rain on St. Mark's, the soil will be parched.

★

Na Jakuba chmury, będą śniegu fury.
Clouds on St. Jacob, wagonloads of snow.

St. Jacob (St. James the Greater) falls on July 25th.

★

Od Świętej Hanki, zimne wieczory i ranki.
From St. Ann's, cool evenings and morns.

St. Ann is the traditional harbinger of fall; her feast falls on July 26th.

★

Wawrzyniec pokazuje, jaka jesień następuje.
Lawrence shows what sort of autumn will follow.

The feast of St. Lawrence comes on August 10th.

★

Jaki dzień Bartłomieja, takiej jesieni nadzieja.
As Bartholomew's Day, so the hope for fall.

St. Bartholomew's falls on August 24th.

★

Jaki Bartek, taki wrzesień, jaki Marcin, taka zima.
As Bart, so September, as Martin, so winter.

★

Na święto Marcina, najlepsza gęsina: patrz na piersi, patrz na kości, jaka zima nam zagości.
For St. Martin's feast, roast goose is best; to know what winter we shall have, look at the bones, look at the breast.

St. Martin's Day falls on November 11th.

*Gdy poździernik ze śniegiem przybieży, na wiosnę długo
śnieg na polach leży.*
If October comes with snow, in the spring snow will
lie long in the fields.

★

Kiedy na Barbarę błoto, będzie zima jak złoto.
Mud on St. Barbara's, winter like gold.

★

Święta Barbara po lodzie, Boże Narodzenie po wodzie.
St. Barbara over ice, Christmas over water.

St. Barbara's Day is December 4th. As with so many
proverbs, we have one which says the exact opposite of
the above:
Niechaj każdy pamięta, jaka Barbara, takie święta.
Let everyone remember: as Barbara, so the holidays.

★

Święta Łuca dnia przyrzuca.
St. Lucy lengthens the day.

St. Lucy's Day falls on December 13th and the winter
solstice is not till December 21st. The proverb must
have originated when the Julian calendar was still in
use; it is known in much the same form throughout
Europe.

★

*Mroźny grudzień, wiele śniegu, żyzny roczek będzie w
biegu.*
Cold December, lots of snow, a fruitful year is in tow.

★

Na Adama pięknie, zima rychło pęknie.
St. Adam bright, winter will soon take flight.

Literally, "winter will soon break." The feast of St.
Adam and Eve is December 24th - Christmas Eve.

★

Wigilia piękna, jutrzenka jasna, będzie stodoła za ciasna.
Christmas Eve fair, the morrow bright, the barn will
be too tight.

— 54 —